PRAISE FOR *YAGUARETÉ V*

"In his stunning debut, the crossroads for Diego Báez in *Yaguareté White* is as much one of the physical Americas as it is linguistic: English, Spanish, and Guaraní converge, clash, and (re)connect through the elusive yet undeniable jaguar who symbolizes 'the souls of all the dead.' Despite diaspora and distance, the speaker tends to the dearly departed as well as the living of his mixed Paraguayan and U.S. roots. Through hard inherent truths—'Everyone knows a man's father / is the first dictator / he must suffer'—and witty takes on 'basic white,' nothing is spared from Báez's exacting yet humorous eye. Through absurdist 'Postcards' from semesters abroad, Google searches, and Gallup polls that reveal a strange obsession with happiness and deference, the speaker unflinchingly reveals the horrors of colonialism and centuries of bloodshed and racism, but not without hope, for the Elusive itself returns to him: the miracle of the lyrical against it all—in the birth of his first child, in which 'her breath first rounded into syllables, / sílabas into word and words into song.' Culturally, critically perceptive yet deeply personal, this is a book you won't be able to put down."

—ROSEBUD BEN-ONI, AUTHOR OF *IF THIS IS THE AGE WE END DISCOVERY*

"A poetry of not knowing: names, origins, where one belongs, how to explain the self to the self, how to explain the self to the other, how to explain to the self the mistranslations and dislocations of movement across languages, borders, hemispheres, and histories. Diego Báez's *Yaguareté White* outlines through a brilliant arrangement and rearrangement of forms so many levels of colonial experience. Through a dissection of whiteness and race, indigeneity and empire, Báez brings us a vision of Paraguay that has yet to be seen in U.S. poetry. In the process, *Yaguareté White*—with its found text postcard poems, its 'dirty language,' its dictionary indexing of Paraguayan and national hierarchies—carves a new place in the poetry of the Americas. This is exciting and innovative work!"

—DANIEL BORZUTZKY, AUTHOR OF *LAKE MICHIGAN*

"In this startlingly fresh debut collection, Diego Báez writes his Paraguayan American experience into and out of focus in smart, combustible poems that confront Latinx whiteness, diasporic return, family dynamics, militarism, and the politics of empire. Stealthily, the Indigenous Guaraní language unsettles English and Spanish in short, punchy, darkly coded jokes ('pukarã') interspersed between lyrics that range from the quotidian to the visionary, and from irony-laced variations on the list poem, the found poem, the prose poem, and the Beat-poet travelogue to compressed couplets and tercets and spare, luminous epigrams in the spirit of Jorge Carrera Andrade. Ever the critic, Báez amps up the cultural and political tensions, yet the lyric voice is vulnerable beneath the brashness, uneasily autoethnographic in its attempt to depict the Other *aquí y allá*, skewering itself and us while breaking down language and allowing us to recompose it again, if only we dare surrender to its tonal and formal shifts. *Yaguareté White* wanders beyond the plains and hills of Paraguay and the flat expanses of the U.S. Midwest, coming across everyone from the poet's ancestors, tourist bloggers, and the dictator's 'goons' to the 'American Marine' and 'basic border anti-immigrant Latinos' in a transnational and transhistorical poetics of personal and social reckoning that is as roar-inducing as it is thought-provoking. Praise the poet poised between the people's tongue and 'My tongue, a bloody muscle, / daggered to la mesa.'"

—URAYOÁN NOEL, AUTHOR OF *TRANSVERSAL*

"*Yaguareté White*, an exceptional debut by Diego Báez, weaves a narrative of belonging, exploring the intricate ties between language and identity. Báez masterfully charts a course between Paraguay and Pennsylvania, illuminating the fusion of languages—English, Spanish, and Guaraní. He refers to this linguistic blend as the 'language of firecracker diacritics,' a vibrant, dynamic mix that encapsulates his experiences. These poems are a testament to the power of language in shaping our sense of self and place in the world. Báez charts a poignant tale of loss, delving into the complexities of national and cultural identity. This is a journey through ancestry of Paraguay, a personal exploration of heritage. One moment depicts an instance of awkward silence with cousins who don't speak English, a silence that eventually 'explode[s] with laughter and handcraft, crudity, horseplay.' This moment is emblematic of the broader themes in *Yaguareté White*, illustrating the challenges and joys of navigating multiple cultural identities. Báez invites readers to reflect on their own experiences of language and belonging through his exploration of loss and a compelling story of belonging, demonstrating the profound connections between language and identity."

—RUBEN QUESADA, EDITOR OF *LATINX POETICS:*
ESSAYS ON THE ART OF POETRY

"With lacerating wit and a fearless commitment to the integrity of the line, Diego Báez explodes the intersection of home, history, and language. I carry these poems with me like a prayer."

—SAEED JONES, AUTHOR OF *HOW WE FIGHT FOR OUR LIVES*

YAGUARETÉ WHITE

Camino del Sol

A Latinx Literary Series

Rigoberto González, Series Editor

Editorial Board

DIEGO BÁEZ

YAGUARETÉ WHITE

POEMS

THE UNIVERSITY OF
ARIZONA PRESS

TUCSON

The University of Arizona Press
www.uapress.arizona.edu

We respectfully acknowledge the University of Arizona is on the land and territories of Indigenous peoples. Today, Arizona is home to twenty-two federally recognized tribes, with Tucson being home to the O'odham and the Yaqui. Committed to diversity and inclusion, the University strives to build sustainable relationships with sovereign Native Nations and Indigenous communities through education offerings, partnerships, and community service.

ISBN-13: 978-0-8165-5219-1 (paperback)
ISBN-13: 978-0-8165-5220-7 (ebook)

Cover design and art by Alan Berry Rhys
Designed and typeset by Leigh McDonald in Landa 11/14 and LL Charlotte (display)

Publication of this book is made possible in part by the proceeds of a permanent endowment created with the assistance of a Challenge Grant from the National Endowment for the Humanities, a federal agency.

Library of Congress Cataloging-in-Publication Data
Names: Báez, Diego, 1984– author.
Title: Yaguareté white : poems / Diego Báez.
Other titles: Camino del sol.
Description: Tucson : University of Arizona Press, 2024. | Series: Camino del sol: a Latinx literary series
Identifiers: LCCN 2023008538 (print) | LCCN 2023008539 (ebook) | ISBN 9780816552191 (paperback) | ISBN 9780816552207 (ebook)
Subjects: LCSH: Hispanic Americans—Ethnic identity—Poetry. | Paraguayans—Poetry. | LCGFT: Poetry.
Classification: LCC PS3602.A386 Y34 2024 (print) | LCC PS3602.A386 (ebook) | DDC 811/.6—dc23/eng/20230426
LC record available at https://lccn.loc.gov/2023008538
LC ebook record available at https://lccn.loc.gov/2023008539

Printed in the United States of America
♾ This paper meets the requirements of ANSI/NISO Z39.48-1992 (Permanence of Paper).

for Sarah

CONTENTS

MOKÕI

MBOHAPY

FOREWORD

THE POEM "A Comprehensive List of Famous Fictional Paraguayans" offers two entry points: it's an indictment of the ways Paraguay has been misused to serve the needs or agendas of others, usually outsiders; and it's a catalog of occasions this South American country, nestled between Brazil, Bolivia, Uruguay, and Argentina, becomes illuminated on the crowded map, singled out. The attention the country receives via these sources is sometimes fleeting or superficial. Yet each item on the list catches the interest of the Paraguayan American speaker, a descendant of an immigrant father, who has a substantive connection to his family's homeland. But when a person is distant from the ancestral home, every small mention or glib reference becomes amplified, perhaps even significant. The poem is a veritable double-edged sword: it spurs the speaker's curiosity and nostalgia at the moment of initial recognition, which eventually turns into disappointment or outrage.

From this cauldron of emotion, a motivation is born: to offer a more respectable consideration of Paraguay's history, languages, and people from the point of view of someone who has experienced the country up close and who continues to visit—via memories and family stories—from far away. Diego Báez, the first Paraguayan American poet to publish a book originally in English in the United States, is in a unique position to pave an important path into a nation and culture that have not received the same level of regard in American letters as its neighboring South American countries and cultures. But make no mistake, he is not presenting himself as a spokesperson or ambassador for Paraguay, though it is likely he will be perceived as such, something that is beyond his control. Like the jaguars in the opening poem that

come to represent
the souls of all the dead. Inseparable from each other,

this people and their origin. So it is, and so am I,
here now in the temple.

Instead, Báez is transparent about his struggles with understanding his own identity: he is of Paraguayan descent, but also has white European ancestry; he didn't grow up speaking Spanish; and the lack of connection to a Paraguayan community in the United States excludes him from the social and cultural foundations that other South American diasporas provide for their respective immigrant populations and subsequent generations. The poem "Autonym" is perhaps the most honest about the adverse effects of dislocation and alienation when the speaker wonders:

We have no idea what they called themselves,
how they referred to each other.

They left no record, no language, no images on walls.
No books of verse survive them, no story and no song

outlived the wash of history, its purgatory curve.

The speaker then imagines his daughter inquiring, "What do we call ourselves?" I believe *Yaguareté White* is the journey toward an answer, but also toward a purpose: to preserve the already precarious threads to a people and land in order to weave them into legacy, an inheritance that "surely . . . had lived there all along," within a larger story that is as important and relevant as those from countries that have had the benefit of robust representation in all media. That resoluteness is what keeps this book intimate, engaging, and personal.

—*Rigoberto González*

YAGUARETÉ WHITE

PETEĨ

YAGUARETÉ WHITE

No jaguars wander my father's village, no panthers
patrol the cane fields caged in bamboo fences,

nestled among the Ybyturuzú, what passes for a mountain
range in Paraguay, the Cordillera Caaguazú. You see,

Spanish adjectives arrive after the noun they describe,
clarifying notes that add color and context.

There is history and then there is history, but there are no jaguars
here, only a pool of blood petrified into stone, a place I call home,

tierra de arcilla, clay so bright it stains orange. This color we call rust in English,
after a chemical reaction used to describe the old, unused, out of practice.

And it's true, no mountain lions roam my mother's home-
town of Erie, Pennsylvania, wasted city of industry, named for the native

people who once combed its shores, called "Nation du Chat"
by the colonizing French, after the region's Eastern Panther.

By now, every oxidizing firearm and spearhead and family
charm has moved west or died out, like the Lynch clan,

my ancestors, or the only indigenous word to survive
the Erie people: "Chautauqua," co-opted by enterprising whites,

literally taken to mean a cross-country, faith-based movement,
a cultural accumulation, which does sound awfully familiar.

Don't worry, because I don't know how to pronounce it either,
the Guaraní. I only know Jopara is like Paraguayan Spanglish,

a mixture of Spanish and Guaraní spoken in the hillside villages,
los campos, the countryside. But I speak none of the above myself.

Even English makes little sense whatsoever, hybrid monster
of predominant whites, but this book is not about albinos.

It's not about willow bark or sugarcane or bartered soil.
It's not about the basilica at Caacupé or the spring of the Virgin Mary,

busy with elbows this morning. It's not about anything
real or true. It's not about binaries, ancient or new.

It's not about a tía teaching her sobrino to speak,
spelling out the sound of each color and pointing:

charcoaled remains of last night's fire, *hũ*.
Ash blown and scattered, *morotĩ*.

It's not about mythology, evil Tau
chasing the child Kerana,

fast silhouette of an immigrant couple
racing across the border, seven offspring in tow,

cursed to haunt the forests outside my father's village.
It's not about a story I only learn online:

the death of Arasy, mother to Rupave and Sypave,
the sun and moon, murdered by celestial jaguars.

The siblings avenged their mother, killing all
but one pregnant jaguar, their end and their beginning.

They are now entangled, twinned. Jaguars come to represent
the souls of all the dead. Inseparable from each other,

this people and their origin. So it is, and so am I,
here now in the temple.

WHAT HAS GONE BEFORE

Past the impromptu photo booth required for entry into Paraguay, past unreadable road signs, past bodegas and alley markets and families hawking ripe mangos by the roadside. Past blown-out tires and tool kits and idling mechanics. Past all of this. Past the white walls of San Juan Diego de Nuestra Señora y la escuela de Sta. Lucía. Past very wide fields without green. Past cattle and brittle burros and children in the road. Past someone we don't know, who waves anyway. Past two men inspecting a snake's corpse with long tools. Past brick walls with broken bottles arranged in rows between the yards. Past the tiny tienda on the corner and somebody's child, another primo maybe, who runs along and laughs. Past the locked, and then unlocked, gate of sugarcane shoots that gives onto Abuelo's land. Past every time I've ever passed, through Customs, through this country, this village, these gates. Past whoever stood here last, under the verdant sun, or the I who understood and asked Abuelo for a blessing.

YOPARÁ

Papi talks with tío Arnulio. Always Arnulio, in Guaraní while tío drives, their language of firecracker diacritics. The drive is not far, but lasts the better part of three hours. One slim lane of asphalt in either direction. We pull over to refuel outside Caacupé. Every visit, we park at these roadside stands to purchase bottles of Pulp and tori of chipá from dark women in blue skirts with gold baskets of bread balanced on their heads. Cousins joined for the ride one time and, as we got older, they began to wait out this drive, to maybe get to know their primos Americanos. We drank soda through neon straws and tore the yellow bread to pieces, the skin of it hard, the warm aroma of butter and corn, sticky with seeds of anise. We couldn't speak then, and they'd learn English eventually, but the silence exploded with laughter and handcraft, crudity, horseplay: retrospect dialing back memory, liquifying every journey in this fictive, lusty sequence.

REGALITO

Some immigrants stuff language into duffel bags like contraband.
Other children never learn to handle the baggage of their claim.

When I ask my father why he didn't teach us Spanish,
he says he tried, but that my brothers and I always squirmed and whined.

I do remember dreading the militant insistence my father
placed on our response to his calls: "Sí, Papi," he'd have us parrot.

Which I guess is a question? Or maybe an affirmation.
Like maybe finding the breathless body of his infant brother

when he was five broke him. So maybe the sound of our voices singing
our inheritance, this tongue of ours, grants a succession of his name, our house.

But I do remember asking my father, more than once, how to say something
stupid in Spanish, like *toaster* or *roller coaster*.

From the driver's seat of that minivan, I'm sure of it, he answered:
"There's not a word for that."

LENGUA

Pink meat sizzles on grates of mortar bricks and metal brackets: blood sausage shanks intestines, lengua, a word for language, loved by my father, red from corralling young calves with Abuelo, smoky, dark now fat around the edges, my father, who ate river fish fresh this morning, who snapped photographs as my uncles slaughtered dinner at dawn, to hear him speak, English at least, to hear him speak of unboned eel and rows of chorizo, but for bistec, pollo, the porcine screams, the parrots cackle—they mock us and sound human—to hear him speak his native tongue at the table, like the only time I heard him in public, Toastmasters '97, nine or ten at the time and mortified, alive now, as we lay Abuelo to rest, alive as Orion deep in purple skies, mis primos trained on tiny limes to slice and squeeze and pluck más from the bower, from the head: "everybody bow," in Spanish of course, a toast, he makes a toast I don't, thunderheads roll in, ash disburses in the breeze, hot orange coals, cold orange cola, Mister, el perro, snaps up scraps when cousins or primas or tía his sister my mother serves tongue to my father, his favorite: fat drips from the grill, flames and the fire snake up this gristle, Father—

grace this meal.

EMPIRE

After the Treaty of Madrid (1750)

History is so many just men
stationed around wide tables
wet lipped and lascivious
sharpening knives and altercating
over which tongue to impale
to their dining plate.

MEN OMITTED FROM THIS MANUSCRIPT

René,
the uncle I never met, because my father found
him dead in his crib or, rather, nestled like a chestnut
between wooden crib and plaster wall.

Tío Arnulio,
who died in the line of duty on the steps of the police station in Villarrica.

Tío Arnulio,
shot on the steps of the police station, right there in Villarrica.

Tío Arnulio,
who we think had unearthed drug runners within the national police, met an early end,
right there in his childhood village of San Francisco Potrero, just outside Villarrica.

San Francisco de Assisi,
per se.

Robert Gramm,
a god-fearing farmer who, along with his wife, Nola, sponsored my father as a high school
exchange student.

Jeff Gramm,
their eldest son, who passed when I was a kid.

Brad Gramm,
their younger son, who passed more recently than I realized. (It's only been ten years.)

All my relations,
from that side of the family.

"That side of the family,"
entirely.

But not my father,
that's for sure.

Or his father,
or his.

But John,
an uncle on my mom's side who divorced his wife when I was a kid and disappeared from
the family for years, only to re-emerge with a new wife and new family and a lease on
life that was really only temporary since he died soon thereafter, the first from that side.
Cancer.

The name John,
from my mother's side, drowned in patronyms and diacritics.

Juan Carlos,
a doctor from Villarrica, who's been married three times so far and invites my father to
every wedding and whose emails included an awful lot of dirty cartoons that I, for some
reason, saw as a kid.

Daniel,
who bit my ear at a nightclub in undergrad.

Everyone
from undergrad.

Nearly all my teachers,
not because they weren't any good, but because only like two of them were men.

A very different kind of calling: José Gaspar Rodríguez de Francia,
at least by name for now.

Augusto Roa Bastos,
because I have nothing to say about him or his talent or legacy.

Augusto Roa Bastos,
because I wanted to read *Yo el Supremo* in Spanish.

Augusto Roa Bastos,
because I couldn't finish it in English, either.

A Paraguayan poet,
whose portrait and statue and museum live in Villarrica and whose name I must always
look up.

Miguelángel Meza, Alberto Luna, and Damián Cabrera
or any other living Paraguayan literati.

The man I will become
when all my translating is done.

SO YOU WANT TO WRITE IN GUARANÍ

After Jayne Cortez via Julian Randall

So you want to write in Guaraní   y
But Papi never told you   y
All you can do is listen / as the tías and the tíos / reminisce, their laughter hissing.

So I Google how to do it   y
I'm running out of time   y
My phone chirps again to let me know that it is dying.

Quick watch a white guy   y
Talk on YouTube   y
Saying isn't it funny / how the children ignore us / but then you say count and they sound like a chorus:

peteĩ, mokõi, mbohapy   y
(And four?)   y
They answer in Spanish / and the missionary man's compassion will vanish.

And he smiles   y
Monetized   y
What can I do but like and subscribe.

POSTCARD FROM YOUR SEMESTER ABROAD, VOLUNTEER TRIP, AND MISSION VISIT

Borrowed from bloggers who post about their visits to Paraguay

I desperately wanted to live in South America. The climate! The food! The beach! One year later, I received a letter signed by George W. Bush himself, inviting me to join the Peace Corps. Of course, I wouldn't have chosen Paraguay myself.

A COMPREHENSIVE LIST OF FAMOUS FICTIONAL PARAGUAYANS

The guy who lied about finding that last golden ticket, much to Charlie and his suspiciously temporarily bedridden grandfather's dismay.

Rosa from Raffi's "Like Me and You" (1985).

Whoever Joey had intended to buy all those weapons from in J. Franzen's *Freedom*, because lord knows no Paraguayan's got his shit well enough together to coordinate an arms deal with an ambitious U.S. teenager awfully reminiscent of Chip, of *Corrections* fame.

And speaking of award-winning novels, like everyone in Lily Tuck's *The News from Paraguay*, though whether these qualify as famous is TBD because, according to Amazon, nobody's read the thing, but def fictional, as Ms. Tuck admitted in her acceptance speech to having never actually visited the country, relying instead on her own marvelous White imagination.

The 19th c. Irishwoman who became "Paraguay's Eva Peron," according to promo material for Anne Enright's *The Pleasure of Eliza Lynch*.

Eduardo Plarr's mom in Graham Greene's *The Honorary Consul*, but even that takes place in Argentina. (The 1983 movie version adopts an unnamed LatAm nation as its politically unstable setting.)

Gary Sanchez, purported inspiration for one of White actor Will Ferrell's production companies.

Owen Wilson's hotel suite's housekeeper in *Bottle Rocket* (1996).

Extras in Michael Mann's remake of *Miami Vice* (2006). Probably.

There's a character with the same name as me in Rebecca Pawel's award-winning *Death of a Nationalist*, but I'd be surprised if he's Paraguayan.

The Carrijura Indians, who exist only in the world of *The White Jaguar* by one William Appel.

Animated idiot hunk Johnny Bravo as the mascot of a sports team called the Capybaras and dressed—correctly, according to the Catholic Church—as a fish.

Whoever was suffering so badly during that drought in The West Wing (S06E16).

A shorter version of this poem rejected by an editor for its brevity.

Argentine novelists like César Aira and Mariana Enríquez, who have perfected the art of co-opting provincial Paraguayan mores. Even Borges escaped his country's restrictions on divorce to wed the daughter of a German immigrant.

Not to mention the weird remnants of an exiled Nazi surgeon in Nueva Germania.

Jenna and George W., the rest of la familia Bush, circa 2006.

All those ambitious bloggers making a go at Making a Difference™.

MARISCAL ESTIGARRIBIA

A small town in the remote western Chaco, site of Dr. Luis María Argaña International Airport

If I had been among the four hundred
enlisted men and women who found themselves
deployed to Paraguay in the summer of 2005,
the first question, for many, would've been:

The fuck, where?

I, of course, know it's sandwiched
between Brasil and the Southern Cone,
this landlocked, peanut-shaped nation
my family has called home.

Soon after, Jenna Bush—of all people—

touched down in Asunción with body-
guards and UNICEF on the agenda.
I could've served in her escort, driven
an armored Chevy Tahoe from the capital,

past los campos, deep into the Chaco's tortured plains,

where her family, too, has taken up residence,
or at least bought a place, a modest ranch on a quiet,
three-hundred-thousand-acre plot, not far from the new
air base down the way.

I could've been there for that, sporting American

military fatigues in the region, not meaning
to re-enact anything, unable to help it.
But who am I kidding? I was in Paraguay
for all the same reasons.

PATRONYM

The first dictator of Paraguay
       —there have been so many—
designed a flag for Paraguay
       with mismatched emblems on each side:

      crouching lion, Phrygian cap;
           palm branch, olive, golden star.
And this particular dictator
       —the trendsetter, OG, precedent—

      drew suspicion for his fondness
           of astronomy and French grammar,
      theodolite directed at the heavens,
           midnight whispers with the elder demons,

    a wizard from the future, surely, such that
        common people of his country
called him by an older name:
        Karaí Guazú,

      "Great Lord" in Guaraní.
           In this, he was neither first
nor alone. Of course, I don't
        know any of this for myself,

    only through the computer
        and my father's few stories
of Stroessner's goons,
        who tortured him and disappeared

so many others. These are repeated
      infrequently,
his tales of interrogation, but the beatings
      are familiar as family.

Everyone knows a man's father
    is the first dictator
he must suffer. Every stayed hand
    a vow to new beginnings,

      a pledge with all the promise
         of a strongman turned soft,
    one who nevertheless lets fly
         the undulating Janus of that two-faced flag.

KARAÍ GUAZÚ

The first Spanish governor of Guayrá, a *criollo* called Hernandarias, born into this New World, a true Americano. It was he who decreed the splitting of Guayrá along its primary waterway, the Payaguá-ý, or "river of the Payaguá." The first creole colonizer carved possession into place like freshwater into clay, the soil so rich it stained his palms red.

Today, scholars recognize the Payaguá to have been a nomadic people of the Guaycurú, known to raid neighboring native farms and colonial encampments alike. But we have no idea what they called themselves, how they referred to each other. How they looked each other in the eye and said: Sister. Mother. Father. Brother.

On the other hand, "Guiacurú," of course,

> an epithet on loan from the enemy

Guaraní to mean *barbarian* or *savage*,

> and the name stuck.

AUTONYM

We have no idea what they called themselves,
how they referred to each other.

They left no record, no language, no images on walls.
No books of verse survive them, no story and no song

outlived the wash of history, its purgatory curve.
But a people's word for *people* often means exactly that,

"a people." Like my daughter, who is one, when she draws
an index finger in the air and points—no shame or malice there—

to paintings, photos, crowds, juguetes,
and with breathy syllables calls them what they are: pee-pol.

I'm reminded the world needs more metaphor,
more rhyme, and greater affinity, more ways to see

our shared traits and struggles, all that persists
across graffitied, cavernous divides.

But when, eventually, she'll turn to me and ask,
"What do we call ourselves?" Then how should I reply?

Are we the X in *Latinx*, the @ in *Latin@*?
Mongrel and mestizo, both. But Americano?

Dios.   Anything but that.

POSTCARD FROM YOUR SEMESTER ABROAD, VOLUNTEER TRIP, AND MISSION VISIT

Borrowed from bloggers who post about their visits to Paraguay

After some initial resistance to learning the language, my fellow Peace Corps volunteers gave in to the draw of Guaraní's dirty words. For instance, the difference between *food* and *small penis* in Guaraní is literally two short syllables: *i'u* and *o'i*.

"Go jerk off on a cactus" is used freely between siblings. And only in Guaraní can the difference between *y* and *u* mean "sex." My homestay family just about died of laughter.

Dirty   dirty   Guaraní

PUKARÃ PETEĨ

Q: Mba'epe ere rako porã paraguaigua?

A: German bush.

KNOCK KNOCK JOKE WITH GOOGLE TRANSLATE

Q: Hey Google.

A: . . .

Q: Hey Goo-

A: *chirp chirp*

Q: Tell me a joke—

A: I'm sorry, that action could not be / completed.

Q: Goddammit. Hey Google!

A: *chirp chirp*

Q: Tell me a joke in Guaraní.

A: . . .

Q: . . .

A: I'm sorry, that action could not be / completed.

Solo: Ejapiro tuna ari!

CALL SOPA SOPA

When I ask for sopa at my grandfather's funeral, Papi hands me soup, and I say, No sopa, and he says, Oh sopa, and trades me the pan of cornmeal, butter and cheese, onions. I say, But in Spanish it's *pan*, and he says, Why not speak Guaraní? But as history has it, Francisco the fool López ordered soup made that way, solid, the way soldiers like a bone with their broth: meatless and fatty, all gristle and sticky. So now whenever anyone asks for sopa it's understood, at least in Paraguay anyway, since that war anyway, the war my grandfather's home country lost on three fronts against three able-bodied enemies, and at least history makes it sound noble by repeating threes in a country of Catholics, that I call sopa sopa and so *pan* must mean something else altogether.

PYNANDÍ I

means the barefooted ones and where they walk

means red soles and dry palms

means green and brown

means naked (nandí) foot (py)

means water from the well and washing at the river

means white men and red women, brown girls and apricot boys

means all the sunny towns of Paraguay

means glass sprinkled like hard candy atop city walls

means cane fields and cane fences

means cane fields on fire

means capybara napping and incessant strays

means yaguareté upriver, underwater, overhead

means termite spires and half-built homes

means the fleet of foot and where they run

means diamond-spackled, wine-splashed skies

means cane reeds and red welts

means cathedrals that melt like wax in the sun

means stars falling like whiskey darkly dropping through sambuca

means surely   all good things must come

POSTCARD FROM YOUR SEMESTER ABROAD, VOLUNTEER TRIP, AND MISSION VISIT

Borrowed from bloggers who post about their visits to Paraguay

In class discussion, ask students to speculate as to why Guaraní is spoken more by rural, less educated, poorer residents of Paraguay and Spanish by urban, more educated, and wealthier citizens. Then circulate recruitment materials for the Peace Corps. Teach them English. Teach them to express gratitude. Teach them. Depart, satisfied by your service.

PYNANDÍ II

Feast of St. John

Tambourines
in his hands

and tambores
in his temples,

the boy danced over
orange-black coals,

& the flesh
bubbled

into blisters,
peeling off

meaty strips
for weeks.

THE SKIN

of a peach
is no longer

Flesh colored, Indian
Red is now

crayon called Chestnut.
Prussia lost her

Blue to Midnight,
and finally in nine-

teen seventy-two
Chartreuse

renamed herself
Atomic Tangerine,

but the promise
of a primrose

is still canary-
colored.

ABUELO DELOUSES MISTER

Rubber hose in one hand,
pumping with the other,
Abuelo douses the poor mutt
in kerosene as Ponchito
and Paola, emerald-bodied
parakeets, shrug shoulders
and fall into fits of laughter,
shaking hands and slapping
one another on the back.
My brothers and I
stand there aghast,
like straight men or suckers.
Like three gringo amigos
made up like mariachis.

ETYMOLOGIES

After Jorge Carrera Andrade

jurumí   *giant anteater*

shy monk go
sweep the monastery you

wide-brimmed
caudillo

                                        toucan

                                        chirps jopará
                                        such   bright orange
                                        berries

tatú carreta   *armadillo*

an armed and armored man
landed, head-down, pebbled, pedigreed
your gentle infantry of one

tubérculo comestible

manioc and yuca
white at the root
meant
to remind
me of something

tapir

it's hard to cast a die
with all the animals
like Pokémon
in Paraguay

aguará guazú   *maned wolf*

fire stalks
stamped out in embers
en inglés: four exclamation marks

yaguareté   *jaguar*

disappeared from the Chaco,
where *-eté* once meant
"real" or "true"

PUKARÃ MOKÕI

Q: Mba'epe ere cervesa porã paraguaigua?

A: German Busch.

MOKÕI

HONEY

So many times, my father has liked to call his boys "honey." He starts, then stops. Catches it short, aborts this instinct, reverts to a masculine familiar, like "sport" or "champ" or "buddy." Buddy. Like some idiot elf. Such an impersonal pleasantry. Such inadequate English.

Buddy was the name of the doll my parents bought Miguel. As the youngest brother, Miguel had begun to act out, attempting to draw attention away from his older siblings. This new doll became my brother's best companion. It also looked remarkably like Chucky from *Child's Play*: red freckles, overalls, the whole bit. I didn't know this at the time, of course (being ten), and only saw Buddy's similarity to the knife-wielding serial killer years later.

What's worse, the only surviving evidence of Buddy is a photograph from the infamous afternoon Miguel—who must have just started to come around to self-consciousness, that age when children begin to lash out at inanimate objects they had believed to be their friends—Miguel had stripped Buddy of his overalls and attacked the fabric body with nontoxic markers, great green and purple streaks. In the photograph, Miguel scowls fiercely, holding the ruined doll upside down. By one leg. A sacrifice or offering.

I imagine my mother laughing behind the lens, amused by this raucous little horror. I assume it was my mother took the picture, since she was home when we were kids. I can't imagine my father knew what to do. Tie loosened, stubble ready for a hot dinner and the local news, confronted with the desecrated corpse of this child's plaything. Maybe he laughed, or said nothing. Maybe he suppressed an anger over the destruction of this store-bought doll. My mother had sewn together stuffed animals for the first two, why spoil this child, the third, his last?

One awful night, one of several, many years later, when adolescents begin to grow beyond themselves, into sharp and angular outbursts, all lank and swagger, Miguel came home drunk and started to fight with my father. They didn't come to blows, not that night, as Miguel could barely stand himself upright. My father ran cold water in the bathroom, stripped Miguel of his jeans and T-shirt, and shoved him in the shower, shouting, struggling to swear in estranged English.

I like to imagine my father washing my brother clean, a tidy parable, a man who comes to terms with the fact of this intoxicated body. Miguel conscious long enough to rinse off or scrub himself drunkenly. My father a flummox of frustration untranslated. Untranslatable, these Americanos of his. Instead, he fled downstairs to finish his whiskey interrupted, pour another. And another. To this day, another. Another.

YUCA

When I turned fifteen

        —no quince for me—

I learned how to drive

        in the family van:

an enormous white   Dodge box on wheels.

Recently my mom claimed I made a big stink

        about how uncool it would be to drive

            to school in that thing, but let me tell you

        I drove that motherfucker   til the wheels fell off.

As a preteen in Paraguay

        —eleven, maybe twelve—

I wolfed down undeboned   fish, I remember

        the white flesh, the way my throat

caught   of a sudden, that quick blade of heat.   But six of my tías

assured me the bone   had only just   scratched my esophagus.

At one white uncle's wedding

        —I must have been eight—

I mistook my dad's glass for apple   juice and then mistook

a sip from the straw. Grandpa Lynch made a comment

for everyone to hear but   it wasn't mali- or salacious,

only a joke   a signal that what I was doing was wrong.

          Of course it had to be my dad's glass,   my mom's dad. And me,

who never liked yuca,
                    the fried stink of it,

                                        an empty starch that sticks in the throat,

even with its white skin   browned to a crisp.

CHESTNUT PEOPLE

Orange skins
corkscrew
in the kitchen.

Little Juancito
calls me "hermano,"
but he's an only child:

cousins   (in English)

      primos   (in Spanish)

          tutyra'y   (in Guaraní)

Son of a single mother,
we're brothers in the kitchen
and his skin is just like mine:

burnished

moreno

pytã

Tanned, we play hide
and seek and learn
to speak by scouring.

POSTCARD FROM YOUR SEMESTER ABROAD, VOLUNTEER TRIP, AND MISSION VISIT

Borrowed from bloggers who post about their visits to Paraguay

After wiping away tears of laughter, our neighbors started to explain the next act. A Cuban dancer, direct from Emboscada, was going to perform. Our neighbor emerged in blackface with a stuffed bosom and posterior, bouncing to a rhythmic drumbeat. She invited men from the audience to join her, tilting her hips to and fro, and J--- responded to the call. He mimicked her exaggerated bouncing up and down. The audience rewarded the pair with jeers, whistles, and applause. I couldn't believe what I was seeing! This would never fly back home.

AMERICANISM

The colonizer kneels, red bandana and denim
alight in October's steepled afternoon.

"This is squash," she says. "We roast
it or boil it and add it to stew."

She cracks it open on her knee,
breaking the skin and exposing

webs of wet seeds, the sticky black
innards of something Rhode Island's

only tribe calls Askutasquash:
a green thing eaten raw.

AMERICANO

My oddest Paraguayan uncle speaks no English and has done very well for himself: big
house, football pitch, spirals of barbed wire, psychotic German Shepherds. He calls me
"Americano," like he's ordering café. I call him "Castellano," but he doesn't get the joke. I
struggle to translate, and helpers serve a tray of biscuits, tea, guava, and margarine. I have
no idea what my uncle does for a living. Coffee or cane sugar, plantations of elder bark way
out en los campos. He has amassed more property, objects, and animals than the rest of
the neighborhood combined. He has bulldozed adjacent lots to expand this private empire.
He has made the most of his time. Never mind the unpeopled rooms and halls, mis primos
off to study elsewhere in the world, boxes of clothing and toys stacked along the walls. His
wife works long hours at the hospital and is never around. The house staff leaves at eight in
the evening, so the night before I fly home, we toast this country's history, we drink to the
memory of anonymous men long gone. We kill the bottle. I don't remember the rest. He
drives me to the airport in the morning, both of us still painfully hung over. Hints of night
vomit occupy the space between us. Then, like two longtime friends who will no doubt
reconnect, he drops me off without ceremony, saying only, "Ciao, Americano." As if it were
another time, a different place. As if that were the end of it.

PASSING THROUGH PANAMÁ, EN ROUTE TO ORD AND UPTOWN, CHICAGO

The only time Miguel and I share the overnight
flight from Asunción Silvio Pettirossi:
land in Panamá around 6 a.m., snag Bloody
Marys at the bar straightaway, sink into a quick
stupor (flight attendants doled out cold canned
refreshments until cutting us off hours earlier),
grab a Subway sandwich, black out, pass
out, wake up to the remains of a demolished footlong,
find Miguel, bag a carton of Duty Free squares,
fail to find anyplace to light them, somehow
locate our gate and make it through the extra security
Copa for some reason requires,
collapse into our seats, nod off, wake up even before
every passenger has boarded, vomit discreetly
into the space between armrest and window,
repeating literally ad nauseum until arrival,
nurse ice chips while Miguel sips grapefruit
juice and chats incessantly with his neighbor,
a guy from Chicago, but not born and raised,
a transplant from the suburbs who's never heard
of Uptown, its inhabitants and sirens, its silences, its animals,
its daily reminders of life's savage chance, the way fortune
will ravage the addict, the unsheltered, the scathed.
Animals like my brother and I who, yes, grab a six-pack before
returning to my apartment on Carmen, only to pass out finally
for real, leaving that last invitation to get truly fucked up unfinished
instead, unlikely lonely totems, the two of us, at the time.

PUNCHLINE

My enterprising uncle—Señor
Castellano—threw a dinner for
me and my dad before we left
again to return again, a circuit
we'd travel again and again.
After aperitifs, I mentioned my
wife's inheritance: her Hebrew
school and parentage. My
uncle's eyes got big, and he
animated into a joke. The only
word I caught, judíos, and I
knew it couldn't end well. But

Years ago, Miguel, age seven, had torn all the pages from the journal I brought to Villarrica for a visit. I shoved him
and straddled and slugged him in the shoulder over and over until I slipped and clocked him clean in the jaw.

he carried on for a while and all
the while I became a fist in my
seat, unfollowing. At last my
uncle rounded the turn to
conclude his wandering pukará.
The joke didn't land, not
because it wasn't funny, who
could say? My dad offered no
utterance, my uncle, palms up,
like *eh?* The entire table's eyes
on me, my face all raised
eyebrows, the clench of my
hands thick with fishhooks,
question marks pinched from
my lips.

FOOTBALL POEM

Paraguay never got its hand-of-god moment, no Diego
Maradona punching his way into the annals,
not a single infamous moment in its sporting history.

SPORTING HISTORY

1992

In the bustling suburbs of Asunción, a human-rights lawyer digging up dirt on former Paraguayan dictator Alfredo Stroessner stumbled upon the extensive and meticulous records of the asshole Pastor Coronel, former head of the formerly secret state police. These immaculate, alphabetized files came to be called los Archivos del Terror, or the Archives of Terror. They document the disappearing, imprisonment, torture, and execution of hundreds of thousands of people across South America during Operation Condor, an internationally orchestrated, information-sharing, prisoner-swapping, wealthy chuckling network of state-sponsored terrorisms. At first, Paraguay, Chile, Argentina, and Uruguay communicated via channels routed through U.S. military bases in Panama, but this lucky lawyer broke the whole thing wide open. And if it weren't for Coronel's fastidious bookkeeping, the whole story would still be under wraps. To be that lawyer, to wield those truths. To see every historiography of the oppressed as a sequence of such happy accidents.

HAʻARÕ·ỸVA FELIZ

Gallup, Inc. asked a thousand people in 148 different countries whether they felt well-rested, had been treated with respect, smiled or laughed, learned something new, did something interesting, or experienced feelings of joy the previous day.

In Paraguay, 85% answered "yes" to all five, landing the nation-state at the very top of that list*

---

* *These metrics omit any mention of starving natives in the Chaco, of street urchins in Asunción and Villarrica, of my abuela's burro, the trembling hembra that's all skin and bones.*

POSTCARD FROM YOUR SEMESTER ABROAD, VOLUNTEER TRIP, AND MISSION VISIT

Borrowed from bloggers who post about their visits to Paraguay

Paraguayans drink yerba mate with both hot and cold water, but most Argentines and Uruguayans would never think of using cold. Paraguayans also differ in their practice of adding yuyos to the water. These can be medicinal or refreshing, and my host brother described how, as a child, his family would send him to the yuyera in the market. Based on how you felt or what you dreamed, the yuyera chose specific yuyos from her supply and prepared them in front of you with a mortar and pestle. I wanted to see this woman work her magic, but when I went to the clinic for a rash, all I got was a tube of calamine.

YUYOS

cashew for good
measure cayenne
and petunias*

---

*Cerca 1540, an indigenous Guaraní woman—Christianized by history as India Juliana— poisoned a
Spaniard with herbs and later bragged about it.*

INHERITANCE

When my child came into this world,
she didn't rock mine or turn it upside down
but flipped it inside out. It felt not like a burning fire,

but like a new chamber opening in my heart,
a fourth dimension unbending
between sternum and spine.

Surely it had lived there all along,
huddled with the Spanish
I hadn't spoken in ages.

Before I was born, my father bought a '57 Chevy:
bright green, gas cap inside one silver tailfin.
Ran like shit. Poured smoke. No seat belts.

My father drove me home from hospital in that thing.
We sideswiped another car on Camelback Bridge in Normal.
Years later, I never learn which party was drunk driving.

I imagine my Spanish is like that green Chevy:
busted, barely runs, a rickety gift.
But that doesn't mean it's not mine to share.

At first, simple whispers suffice:
words for "love" en Guaraní y Español.
How those early endless hours

—then days and weeks—
balloon, uninvited, to encompass the story
I tell myself of her genesis.

The way a point turns to line,
a line to surface, surface to volume,
until all that's left is time.

That first long year, when we moved
so seldom, estacionados en la mecedora.
Like a landslide, these evening rocks

roll into crawling, a crawl to first steps,
her carriage precarious until the wild,
grinning child turns to run.

And I see her already,
moving through timelines I no longer recognize.
An anchor point or past tangent,

I'm already a bystander
in the green blaze of her ascendent arc.
She has changed so much—so much of me—already.

She fills space, and grows, and will not stop
growing, god willing. With hope, Hashem,
she'll continue to move

in pursuit of her futures,
not any one in particular, but all of them
simultaneously

unfolding like tesseracts
outside the quickly shrinking cage
of a father's captive heart.

Because wasn't it just yesterday
her breath first rounded into syllables,
sílabas into word and words into song?

Was it not just yesterday
she fit inside the makeshift cradle of my arms,
not yet so far removed from this vast world she'd cracked wide open?

It's certain only to quicken.
I see her climb into that bright green Bel Air
destined to face whatever fate alights:

to swerve away or embrace, to box, to bridge
the distance between her now and future self,
to mind the road for other lives unwinding.

Of course, all this unfolds in the time it takes to fall asleep,
to sway in the morning sun after a restless night,
her head on my shoulder, something with rhythm on the radio.

I imagine if there's an afterlife worth living for,
it's probably this, just like this, forever.

MBOHAPY

EL PAPA

A quiet boy, Juan Pablo points to a paper savior he drew, lighted blue in the kitchen's window, insects pinned like specimens to the white stucco walls, his boy's body, only head and hands above the table, laughter lashes like thunder (the clinking of glasses and spirits still decanting); eyebrows black, eyes full of irises (the smoky smell of bistec searing); he won't grow up to be a preacher like his father, but smiles like a stoic: a very young version of the man he will become; his father's darkness, his mother's stillness; the boy at last smiles but uncomfortable still, eyes on us strangers, his primos, Americanos, like strangers, silent beneath a prized photograph of his own devout father: face bowed, palms together, the actual Pope signing a cross in the air.

CAPYBARA OUROBOROS

Forgiven as a fish
by 16th-century Jesuits,
who feared the natives

would starve to death
during Lent,
I can't help

but picture
this overgrown
guinea pig

half-swallowed
by a green anaconda:
black feet and webbed

toes protruding
from the gaping O,
its tail a tongue

flicking at the end
of an animal that could
only be a rodent

forced down the throats
of locals who did, indeed, starve
in the end, for centuries.

So now the capybara bathe
en el centro de Villarrica
beneath a statue of a poet

who isn't me, and never will be,
whose work I haven't read,
and whose name I do not know.

If this must be a metaphor
for anything, it's this:
the dead end of history   .

is neither serpent nor rodent,
not meat or fish, man or monument,
but each masquerading as the other.

SPECIAL DRAWING RIGHTS

Imagine the young boy perched,
cross-legged, sketchpad in hand, a gift
from his grandfather, this free time to bring
daydreams into deep color, an iron cannon in Cantigny
Park, suburban green space named after a battle in France.

At the time, in that present, Grandpa unpacked
a picnic of brown bags, carrot sticks and sandwiches,
an apple, a cookie, the wartime rose on his forearm
fading to a dark blur, flesh burnt into service.

Whereas nation-states purchase these baskets of currencies,
securing their position in the hazard constituencies of history,

I carry a reserve of foreign exchange assets:
Abuela in her kitchen, shaded by mango and lime
bowers, a tin shack and brick oven out back,
not the big addition with plumbing and gas line,
electricity and cell coverage, a solid four bars by the pigsty.

So I must remit myself back into this picture,
what the grandfather fought for, this momentary freedom,
what the boy rendered as just another pretty garden—
a war weapon, a memory.

AMERICAN MARINE

It's not a minivan's bumper sticker
advertising Semper Fi, not the neighbor boy,
or your nephew, tu sobrino, not that former classmate,
the poor kid with something to prove,
this radiating bruise, these fields of green,
the browns and blacks, such multitudes of white.

And it shall prove forever faithful,
this unflagging azure, yours and mine,
bound as we are to this shameless,
star-spangled cerulean, this fast bruto,
these young men, their midnight commerce,
a steely, certain sheen to their bright sacrifice.
This acidic sapphire, this oceanic empire,
this bleeding stump, this cyanide.

HIMMELBLAU

The ex–German officer and his Argentine wife
arrived just after five and not a moment too soon:

a magnetic chess set askew on the bed, daylight
whitening every black space on the board.

Asunción will steal your breath away
but not before your past catches up to you

and pales in comparison. The way a word
can never check its baggage at the border.

PUKARÃ MBOHAPY

Q: Mba'epe ere guariñi porã paraguaigua?

A: . . .

NUEVA GERMANIA

Way out in the campo, rumors of twins and albinos, fugitives camped out for decades, protected by that sympathizer Stroessner. Never near enough Villarrica to notice, save mysteriously wealthy Mr. Friedman, the cane magnate who paid for my dad's first flights to Gridley, Illinois, who went on and on about radioing German submarines off the coast of South America using the conspicuous tower planted in his backyard.

At the time
I suspected
his surname,
which sounds German
(and is!), but it wasn't until I began to raise a child, who is Jewish,
that I came to understand Mr. Friedman may have been hunting prey, not conspiring
with underwater enemies. But my child, who will never ask her bisabuelos for a blessing (QEPD),
still must face a country collapsing in on itself from the weight of its own freighted history
of hate that I say in the final analysis it's time again to return fascists to pasture.

SAN FRANCISCO POTRERO

The stone eroded and seems to sag without sinking, chirrup of crickets and frogs and a wrought iron gate that wants to be perpendicular. But isn't. A congregation of horseflies at dawn surveying fresh compost: the lingering aroma of orange rind. The tomb's illusive lowering looks like that of a riverbed disappearing in a downpour along a bad stretch of back road, rendering the mausoleum's marble stature heavy and flagging with overgrown green in the eyes of the two women who shuffle in from the campo's ragged edge, arriving veiled and cane white and arthritic of wrist, begging for the passage of a long dead relative at the boundary of the black gate's cant, sagging painfully lower and lower each morning in these days before Advent, both of them wishing the other would edge near enough to peer in or pluck the dead moss and brown petals from the stone.

ON THE ANNIVERSARY OF THE SECOND FOUNDING OF BUENOS AIRES

December 1990

Four hundred years ago, my father
stopped over in Argentina for a weekend,
drawing his boys downriver from that Mother of All Cities,

la Nuestra Señora Santa   María de la Asunción,

to reconquer this abandoned backwater
outpost, this city of sweet air, reviving the colonial
headquarters for a second coming, a new lease, a sequel, or maybe

it's more like rebooting the franchise.

A lifetime later, when his son returns, para su luna de miel,
the kind trans salesperson hawking keychains in Caminito
can only roll eyes at the newlywed Americano couple.

These are not the Paraguayan mestizos

who forged down the River Paraná like oddities,
outliers, their departure from a mecca
nestled in the northern forests. Four hundred and ten years ago,

forty years was a lifetime. But a metropolis doesn't rot

in the pampas. It only longs for inhabitants and more
than pythons in the trees or jaguars underwater,
it's the fleet-footed ones, their spears and squawks,

that drive away outsiders, prevent settlement, until, that is,

fair winds won the day. Traders called it the "Paris of South America."

A strange comparison. Parisians had been minting
gold for nearly two millennia. Even after Algeria, the French

Republic persists, Roma and North Africans dancing in its streets,

hustling for change, with so many native
women perched on plastic tarps, casting Chinese
trinkets for double price in blue dollars.

MOM PUTS MIGUEL'S TWO-WEEK SENTENCE FOR DUI IN PERSPECTIVE

Remember when
we used to go
to Paraguay

for weeks
without
so much

as a single
phone call
to let any-

one know how
the trip went
and every-

one always was
always so kind
and took care but

no child
of mine
should spend

even small time
behind
bars in county,

and don't you
remember
how we'd all

go together and
the first week always
felt like forever?

ENGLISH EVENTUALLY

An editor asks for more
Guaraní in the manuscript.

I transcribe—by hand—
every word of Avañe'ẽ I know:

Haku. "Hot."
Cambu.

(Kamby)
"Milk." (Or

"cow,"
more like?)

Also *y*,
for "water,"

which does not exist
in English

(the sound for water
in Guaraní).

But in Spanish *y* is "and" so
why is Guaraní for "water"

the same as "and" in Spanish?
And who   knew *Guaraní*

is "Avañe'ẽ" in Guaraní?
Not I.

(The sound for water
in Guaraní.)

I call it the language of man only
when I go to revise and see

haku and kamby, mba'
éichapa.

Atop a dry tree,
a malnourished crow pigeon.

My tongue, a bloody muscle,
daggered to la mesa.

THE ASSUMPTION OF WHITENESS

It's not so unusual for a young boy
to experiment with his mother's dress:
heels and pearls, all the cute paraphernalia
Hallmark has the courage to depict in sweet
sepia on its greeting cards one aisle over at the Walgreens.

Even more common is the purchase by a nurse,
the mother of a young boy, of Clinique green
tubes of flesh-colored concealer,
key to hiding the bright red blotches on her late-
blooming child's budding chin cleft.

Still, is it strange for a preteen in Normal,
Illinois to deflect the question from classmates:
"Are you wearing makeup?" He said it was a medicine,
this application of a basic white. But the girls knew better:
boys always mistake concealment for a cure.

BASIC WHITE

basic white is so basic right

basic white is doublespeak for supremacy

basic white enshrines individual liberty

basic white lives for private property

basic white takes what it wants when it wants it

basic white bleeds what it needs to survive

basic white includes you if you like

basic white j'adores yoga, tacos, head dressings

basic white buys overpriced merchandise from its sports teams

basic white hangs Indians, Redskins, and Braves on its racks

basic white calls basic white business back

basic white hosts the Zoom call, crowdsources, starts up

basic white cowork, happy hour, foosball

basic white tablet, dual screen, laptop

basic white salary, medical, and dental

basic white annual, physical exam

basic white braces and corrective lenses

basic white migraine the size of a school bus

basic white blue light, lens flare, flare up

basic white medicate and basic white smile

basic white hits send on the Outlook invite

basic white agenda, action item, KPI

basic white makes the ask, gauges bandwidth, talks offline

basic white Excel, boss border Nextel

boss white women echo one another in the boardroom

boss white echo chamber pats back repeatedly

basic white charity 5K with your colleagues

basic white down payment, mortgage, auto loan

basic white Tesla, crossover, hybrid

basic white push for renewable energy

basic white windmills, solar, geothermal

basic white thinking globally, acting locally

basic white runs for the school board, platform

basic white can have it all, trust me, go hard

basic white heavy-duty stroller on the sidewalk

basic white post-brunch chat right there in the bike lane

basic white drives an empty SUV in the carpool

basic white flocks to pan flutes in the food court

basic white (Chardonnay!) while you grocery shop

basic white book club, knitting circle, prayer group

basic white road rage, office party, lynch mob

basic white show trial, witch hunt, red scare

basic white scapegoat, undocumented, disappeared

basic border anti-immigrant Latinos in Texas

basic border anti-immigrant Latinos in Florida

basic white Cruz and basic white Rubio

basic white stock trade, initial public offering

basic white margin call, basic white valuation

basic white stock dilution, miscegenation

basic white states' rights, deregulation

basic white Offspring, ska, swing, and new wave

boss border rock 'n' roll, rap, jazz, and disco

basic white Apostolic, Mennonite, Mormon

boss border pagan, native, unknown

basic white rally in Charlottesville, Virginia

basic white road rage in Charlottesville, Virginia

basic white vigil in Charlottesville, Virginia

basic white lack of basic human empathy

basic white sees things as things not themselves

basic white pivots, disrupts, reinvents

basic white frat house on Cinco de Mayo

basic white frat house on Halloween night

basic white frat house made its way to the White House

basic white power, the privilege, the burden

basic white lone wolf, militia, they'll murder you

basic white chambers of commerce downtown, Doric white columns and sculpted facades, like continental halls of government, like Grecian temples to the gods

basic white myth of basic white Western Civ

basic white invention of the Orient, the East

basic white invention of the boss white race

boss border come up on you straight rocking whiteface

GRACE BAPTIST

basic white minivan in the Baptist Church parking lot,
lurching forward then jerking to a halt,
immediately following the massive annual Christmas pageant,
Mom sliding open the side door, 100% certain
it's Papi and my brothers inside

a simple mistake, one family for another:
three brothers, a father and mother. As if there's ever been
a better metaphor for divorce: a car that looks exactly like yours
cracked open on accident, everyone illuminated by that familiar
dome light, on each face the same expression:
you're not who I thought you were

LYNCH CHRISTMAS

My uncle—my white uncle—
built me an Amnesty House.

I lived there, in the gingerbread,
ice white frosting, black licorice

barring white windows,
Life Saver over the entrance.

Come on, of course
you have to laugh, my uncle—

my white uncle—says.
Yuck yuck and hardy har.

It's all fun and games, not directed at me,
because Papi came over the right way:

plane ticket, scholarship, host family.
Passport stamped Asunción, Miami, Chicago.

My father plucked sesame seeds off his hamburger bun.
He thought they were fungus or bugs.

He never really got along with my uncle
—my white uncle—the one who built me

the Amnesty House, where I lived,
downstairs, for a while.

MANGER MADE BY HANDS

Christmas is trees in my dad's backyard, except we never called him Dad, only Papi, and never graduated to Papá because no one else in the neighborhood spoke Guaraní on the phone hella loud, exhausting calling cards, punching in strings and strings of digits scribbled on scratch paper, stuck to the fridge. But it's my father driving his young family into what passes for woods in Central Illinois to fell an evergreen in December, after snow has fallen for days. It's not a manger made by hands how they do in the hottest months of summer in Asunción, silly tacky icons and tinsel and blinking lights, hard candy and prayer cards, midnight vigils, Spanish Mass. But yes. My dad's the brown guy on the block now in Bloomington who leaves his lights up well into July.

LUNA DE MIEL

For Sarah

Luna looming like one yellow wedge
of a ripening orange we'd bought
at the market just up from the beach.
I tell you, I know where we're going.

We become irretrievably lost.
Loaded down with groceries, one wrong foot
from that lone market's fluorescent mouth,
dusty roads and endless rows of candy-painted cabanas,

completely invisible in the unelectrified dark of this virgin night.
Had we become cursed to wander the rainforest
like Tau and Kerana, whose story ends
poorly for the lot of them, I'd imagine?

I don't know how their story ends,
because I didn't learn it in school,
or at home, or from friends.
Mi media naranja, under this moon

made of god's own golden honey,
I learned it from you.
You wanted me to make this poem
about the restaurant we finally found,

my rusty Spanish to get directions,
to be a good man, to husband and groom.
And we did wind up back at the rental,
sweaty and deadened, but I remember:

the tawny astronomy of your skin,
celestial jaguars submerged in deep sky.
A future cast by a star so bright
only you could've conjured it.

KNOCK KNOCK JOKE IN GUARANÍ
FOR A GROWING CHILD

Q: Knock knock.

A: Who's there?

Q: Rohi.

A: Rohiwho?

Duet: I love you, too!

PORTRAIT OF THE ARTIST WITH CLUBFOOT

para mije Sanna

If it's true my bisabuelo suffered double club-
feet, hobbling the hot streets of Villarrica,
straw hat in hand—

And if it's true Abuelo's chicken legs bore
the weight of ten mouths to feed by a ragged, time-
scorched life thrashed by sun and cane—

Then my father must brandish a scar the length of his shin,
a wound familiar to immigrant farmworkers
or immigrants who worked on farms

before they sacrificed scythe for spreadsheet,
sugarcane for insurance claims.
Then I, too, must always walk intoed,

like a toddler or paloma, braces on my feet
the moment I entered this English-speaking
world. And you, my child, how will you move

past the past and through all of your fathers?
On py broken by chance and blood?
or nandi and longing as the day you were born?

May the bright red blazon of your left sole's birthmark
light your feet aflame. Plant these steps, your first few,
firmly on this oxidizing earth. Let it inherit you.

NOTAS

"Yopará"

A conversational combo of Spanish and Guaraní spoken throughout Paraguay, like Spanglish, among many, here in the States.

"Empire"

The Treaty of Madrid demarcated colonized lands claimed by the Portuguese and Spanish in what became South America. The treaty called for the evacuation of the Indigenous Guaraní. Resistance led by Sepé Tiaraju culminated in the Guaraní War (1754–56), which could only ever end with the slaughter of 1,500 natives, including Tiaraju—an eventual halving of the native population—and the forced relocation of survivors.

"Men Omitted from This Manuscript"

The Paraguayan poet whose likeness graces the museum in Villarrica is Manuel Ortiz Guerrero (1894–1933). Living Paraguayan literati include Susy Delgado, Mia Castagnino, Renée Ferrer de Arréllaga, Alba Eiragi Duarte, and others, I'm sure.

"So You Want to Write in Guaraní"

The word for water in Guarani (y) sounds like a lighthearted, u-shaped grunt.

"Mariscal Estigarribia"

Field Marshal José Félix Estigarribia (1888–1940) commanded Paraguay (backed by Royal Dutch Shell) to victory over neighboring Bolivia (backed by Standard Oil) during the Chaco War (1932–35). Seventy thousand civilians died. Paraguay unearthed zero salable oil in the Chaco it won in the war.

Dr. Luis María del Corazón de Jesús Dionisio Argaña Ferraro (1932–99) served as a judge during the military dictatorship of Alfredo Stroessner, during which the torture, murder, and disappearance of Paraguayan civilians became commonplace.

"Postcard from Your Semester Abroad, Volunteer Trip, and Mission Visit"

"Go jerk off on a cactus" translates to "Ejapiro tuna ari" in Guaraní.

"pukarã peteĩ"

"What do you call good Paraguayan women?"

"Call Sopa Sopa"

Francisco Solano López (1827–70) was the second President of Paraguay, appointed after his father, the first President of the Republic, passed away. López the Second is best known for instigating the War of the Triple Alliance (1864–70), which saw Brasil, Uruguay, and Argentina allied against Paraguay. By many estimates, the war killed nearly 70 percent of Paraguay's men. López himself was assassinated, which finally ended the onslaught.

"pukarã mokõi"

"What do you call good Paraguayan beer?"

"Americanism"

The Narragansett are the only federally recognized tribe in Rhode Island, but the lands served also as home to the Seaconke Wampanoag, Pokanoket, and Mashapaug Nahaganset, among others.

"Yuyos"

Cashew, *cayenne*, and *petunia* all share roots in Tupí, a language long diluted, all its speakers disappeared, Guaraní one of several distant descendents.

"Special Drawing Rights"

Refers to an obscure international currency used for balancing debts between sovereign nation-states.

"American Marine"

Dedicated to the twenty veterans of the U.S. armed forces who will take their lives today.

"Himmelblau"

German for "sky blue."

"pukarã mbohapy"

"What do you call good Paraguayan warriors?"
Incidentally, Germán Busch (1903–39) served as an officer during the Chaco War and, later, as President of Bolivia. During his brief presidency, Bolivia nationalized Standard Oil, created a labor code, and opened its borders to unfettered Jewish immigration, the only country in the world to do so at the time. Sadly, the immigration thing caused a scandal, and the whole operation backfired. He quickly declared a dictatorship and then killed himself. He had tried to end his life twice before, while yet a cadet in the Bolivian military.

"Nueva Germania"

Small town in rural Paraguay, founded in 1887 by German anti-Semites, Bernhard Förster and his wife, Elisabeth Förster-Nietzsche (sister to the famed philosopher), one of several such colonies to spring up. Mengele himself resided in the village of Hohenau during the 1950s, under the reign of brutal dictator Alfredo Stroessner.

"Mom Puts Miguel's Two-Week Sentence for DUI in Perspective"

Only the imagined Miguel of this manuscript served time for a DUI.

"English Eventually"

Like many peoples, the Guaraní referred to their own words and phrases, their expressions and idioms, their patois and parlance, as, simply, "the language of man" or "the people's tongue."

AGUYJE

RIGO, PARA todos. Todos. Y todos.

Rosebud, for your words and encouragement, your trust and your ear, your brilliance and your friendship. Thank you.

Geoff and Derek, for enough to fill my cup many times over. For such close reads, and good times, and hard conversations. Geoff, especially for naming the apophatic. Derek, especially for your actually endless font of references and shelf draws.

Mike Theune, for suggesting a radically different order so very early on. And for repeating the phrase "negative capability" enough that I found myself forced to absorb it, on levels I could not have otherwise named.

Peter, for the counsel and conversation. For sharing in cinema, my friend! For refusing to authorize *The Flaneur of South Boulevard*. I'll get those permissions yet.

Mi familia a Surge. The Emergents, in particular. Thank you, Carmita, for the best interview experience to this very day. Cecily, for pouring yourself into each of us. Tamara, for your energy and aura, your magic.

Every CantoMundista. What imperfect, problematic, incredible Latinidad we inhabit and perpetuate. I want to build a future with you all.

The Stephen and Tammy Lynch Home for Wayward Nephews. I had nowhere to land, and you welcomed me. Thank you.

Armando and Miguel, there's no way I'd be who I am without you.

Papi, for loving us in ways you were not shown. That act of translation lives with me always. Siempre. Gracias.

Mom, for printing and binding my high school poems at Kinko's. You were the first person to teach me that some things are worth holding onto to cherish.

Sarah, I could not have created this without you. You are so generous and so patient and kind. Thank you for lending your ear and your eye and your heart all the time. I hope only to uphold the vows we remake every day anew. I am so fortunate to meet fate with you. TQM TMN.

CREDITS

"Yaguareté White," *Freeman's* and *Latino Poetry: A New Anthology* (forthcoming)

"What Has Gone Before," *RHINO Poetry*

"Regalito" and "Lynch Christmas," *Acentos Review*

"Lengua," *ANMLY*

"Call Sopa Sopa," *Luna Luna*

"Pynandí" and "El Papa" (as "Juan Pablo"), *Ostrich Review*

"The Skin," *Ampersand*

"Americanism," *Flatmancrooked*

"American Marine," *The Rumpus*

"Himmelblau," *Columbia Poetry Review*

ABOUT THE AUTHOR

DIEGO BÁEZ is a writer, educator, and abolitionist. He is the recipient of fellowships from CantoMundo, the Surge Institute, and the Poetry Foundation's Incubator for Community-Engaged Poets. He has reviewed books for *Booklist, Harriet Books*, and the *Boston Globe*. Other writing has appeared or is forthcoming in *Freeman's*, the *Georgia Review*, and *Latino Poetry: A New Anthology*. He lives in Chicago and teaches at the City Colleges.